The United K   on

United Kingdom Reading Association

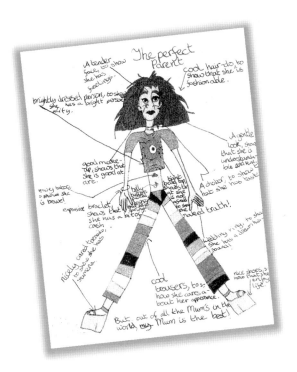

Children's Writing Journals

By Lynda Graham and Annette Johnson

End piece by Eve Bearne

Minibook 16

CONTENTS

Dedications:

For Martin, and for our grandchildren:
Ainsley, Joel, Jessica and Isabel
(Lynda)

For my Dad Peter Leonard Tappin
(Annette)

INTRODUCTION
Lynda Graham

For a number of years now, primary teachers in Croydon have engaged in collaborative action research projects about the teaching of reading and writing. In the first year of the Croydon Writing Project (Graham 2001) one of the teachers - Annette Johnson - created and introduced a social model of writing journals in her Y6 classroom (Johnson 2000). The children in Annette's Y6 class achieved remarkable success as writers. At the end of the two-term research module all children (including formerly inexperienced writers predicted a level 2/3) achieved at least a level 4 in their English SATs, and a significant number achieved a level 5 (including many who had been predicted level 4). Inspired by this success, a number of teachers chose to introduce a similar model of writing journals in their classrooms. In some classes the journals became central to children's development as writers. In others they did not, and the teachers found writing journals difficult to manage. Because of these different responses we decided to set up a specific project about writing journals.

We invited experienced teacher researchers from the Croydon Reading and Writing Projects (Graham 1999, 2001, 2002) to join us, and were pleased that our eleven volunteers ranged from teachers of Reception to Y6. This allowed us to study writing journals across the age range. The Writing Journal Project teachers were: Carol Domingo (Reception), Irene Napier (Y1), Sarah Hayward (Y1/2), Gaynor Talley (Y2), Joanne Greenhalgh (Y3), Pat Parlour (Y4), Vivienne Esparon (Y5), Kim Lawrence (Y5), Jenny Llewellyn (Y6), Linda O'Callaghan (Y6) and Annette Johnson (Y6). The research period was for two terms. Each teacher kept a reflective journal and made observations of four carefully chosen case-study children.

We chose case-study children who were representative of the class in terms of their gender, ethnicity, writing ability and attitude to writing. (For a more detailed explanation see Graham 2003). We met regularly in after-school meetings and discussed ways of managing writing journal sessions and pupil progress, with particular reference to case-study children. I made scribbled notes of each discussion, and these were then typed and sent to the teachers. Eve Bearne accepted our invitation to be critical friend to the project, and we were delighted that she joined us throughout the year in spoken and written conversations about our research. An application to UKLA for a research grant was successful, and enabled teachers to meet for a whole day with Eve at the end of the project, to talk and write about their research.

We measured children's progress as writers in the Writing Journal Project using CLPE Writing Scales (Barrs 1996). We had previously used these scales to assess children in the Croydon Writing Project (Graham 2001, 2002). CLPE Writing Scale 1 was used for Y1, Y2, and Y3, and CLPE Writing Scale 2 for Y4, Y5 and Y6. Children were assessed at the beginning and end of each two-term project module. In the first three years of the Croydon Writing Project children made good progress as writers; an average 72% moved on at least one level on the CLPE Scale in every two-term module. Children in the Writing Journal Project made exceptional progress. In the same two-term period, 80% moved on at least one level on the CLPE Writing Scale. It seems that the introduction of writing journals contributed to this progress.

The key features of Annette's model of writing journals (Johnson 2000) are:
1 Time is allocated within the school day for the class to work in journals. Teachers plan two or three whole-class sessions a week, each lasting 20-30 minutes. Although in some classes children choose to take journals home, regular whole-class time is central to the success of writing journals.
2 Children choose what to write and draw in their journals.
3 Children are invited to choose where to sit, and are encouraged to work with friends if they so choose.
4 Children decide whether to share journal entries with the teacher and other children. Many choose to do this, but some entries are private, and this privacy is respected.
5 Children themselves take responsibility for their journal entries. The journals are not written dialogues between teacher and pupil. Teachers do not respond with written comments, nor do they mark journal entries. This is in contrast to models of reading journals described by Street and Barrs (1998), and writing journals described by Hall (1989) and the National Writing Project (1990).
6 At the end of each writing journal session, time is given for volunteers to share work with the class. This is central to the success of writing journals. Ideas for journal entries spin across the classroom, and children develop a real sense of themselves as writers in a community of fellow writers.

Our minibook begins with a chapter *Why writing journals?* in which Annette explains why she introduced her model of writing journals. An analysis of how her Y6 children used writing journals follows, in *What I found* (chapter 2). In *Organising writing journal sessions* (chapter 3) I outline ways in which the Writing Journal Project teachers managed journal sessions and in chapter 4, *Should I let them draw?,* Annette discusses the issue of drawing in writing journals. Finally, in chapter 5, *Writing like writers,* I describe the ways in which case study children wrote like writers in their writing journals. We are delighted that Eve Bearne accepted our invitation to write an End Piece, and thank her for her advice and encouragement throughout the Writing Journal Project.

Chapter 1
WHY WRITING JOURNALS?
Annette Johnson

Anyone who wants to start writing journals with their own class needs to understand the reasoning behind how a writing journal session is organised. My model developed as a result of teacher action research. The primary benefit of action research is that it allows the classroom teacher to ask fundamental questions about learning environments and classroom practices, to introduce new ideas, be creative and to take risks. My initial research question was: "How can I help children, particularly boys, to become competent and confident young writers?"

Children's reading and writing histories
Our previous work on reading (Graham 1999) had shown that children who were failing to meet expected academic levels often had negative and alienating memories of their early reading experiences with adults. We introduced group reading, paired reading, literature circles (King 2001) and friendship reading to support social and emotional interaction around reading. At the start of the Writing Project I decided to seek pupil histories about both reading and writing. The results were surprising: while 75% of the children demonstrated a positive attitude towards their reading experiences, only 10% of the same children described positive or happy associations in their writing memories.

The majority of children within my class associated the writing experience with incompetence or anxiety; even those children who were perceived by me to be able writers did not consider the experience to be emotionally rewarding.

Finding a personal writing voice
This was a fundamental realisation. Children who were competent within their literacy skills, who met their targets, who could write successfully in a variety of genres, failed to express any sense of joy in their written achievements other than via recognition, by the teacher, of an improvement in writing skills:

"My handwriting is getting better...I can spell more words, without making so many mistakes...I can write more than a page now" (Rebecca Y6)

I knew the children had an increasingly sophisticated knowledge of the writing features of different genres and could write in the style of various authors, but there was an aspect of the literacy process that was missing: the creative enjoyment of personal choice. The children in my classroom were writing for me and for the curriculum, not for themselves. Moreover, less able children, whose literacy skills were under-developed, found writing a totally alienating experience.

The National Literacy Framework (DfEE 1998) is the main strategy for teaching English within the primary classroom. It is thorough, comprehensive and well organised, providing plans to teach the necessary skills for reading and writing and to introduce different literacy styles and genres. However it under-develops one aspect in the development of young writers: the need to experiment and "play" with the child's personal writing voice.

Children's own writing language

The one literacy lesson that did motivate the entire class and helped create a true community of writers was poetry. Free-verse, experimental expressions, no worries about the rules of grammar and punctuation; poems which can rhyme in some places and stop short in others; poems which allowed children to record their own ditties, sayings they hear at home, raps they chant in the playground. Many will recognise the bustle of children sharing their ideas – charged by the undercurrent energy of "flow" (Csikszentmihalyi 2002).

Recording the differences in class climate and atmosphere during a poetry lesson I noted:
  • the absence of concern about making syntactic mistakes;
  • the use of personal language, as spoken by the children;
  • the fun and community from sharing written work.
During poetry sessions I felt my goal, to encourage competent and confident young writers, was achieved. A key difference was the inclusion, and writing, of the children's own language and the opportunity to share this language with their peers.

Children's own language comes from their home, their peer groups, their school environment and the popular media; it all combines and evolves into what may be called their linguistic cultural capital (Bourdieu 1977). Children's own language is what children say, what they hear around them and what circles around inside their heads. Children's own language is dynamic and in a constant state of flux: words, sayings, figures of speech, quotes from songs, books, films, video games, television programmes and adverts. Children's language is real language, for them.

Beginning writing journals

Opportunities for children to write about interests that hold personal power and fascination, and to write in the words and phrases of their own language, are rare in the English curriculum. The literacy framework focuses on chosen texts to demonstrate the characteristics of the genre to be taught. In my reflective journal I wrote:

> *"While it is the norm for children to respond positively to well-written text, the possibility for creative autonomy of choice and style within the independent writing session fits awkwardly in the arrangement."* *(Johnson 1999)*

Children needed time to reflect, to revisit their writing, time to play with and create phrases, time to research links, time to read aloud and time to think. I felt the lack of both time and the opportunity for personal choice within writing was a fundamental barrier to creating confident young writers. I decided to timetable a new activity into the English curriculum: one that would provide time to play with writing. This came in the form of writing journals. I envisaged the writing journal as a type of notebook in which the child could write about hobbies and interests and experience a real freedom in writing. Children could write their own choice or words and phrases, experience the pleasure of playing with language and the power of sharing it with their peers.

In writing journals, children could be reflective and independent in their choice of subject matter and could work socially with a favourite partner or group to create writing communities. At the end of each writing journal session children could, if they wished, share their writing with the class community. Controversially, I would not mark the writing journals. All other writing was marked and evaluated by me; this would be the children's own writing book, free from comment or judgement, an opportunity to explore writing without interference. Writing journals would provide the time to play, and have fun, with writing.

Chapter 2
WHAT I FOUND
Annette Johnson

Writing journals provide the opportunity, the space, and the learning community that enables children to find a personal writing voice. I discovered that children needed to capture, replicate and celebrate texts that they had heard, spoken or read elsewhere. Songs, poems, chants and catchphrases from the home, playground and media are all recorded in writing journals. Their presentation is often elaborate and carefully copied, shared with friends and peers and stored within the pages of the journal to be re-read later. These texts are expressions of the inner voices of the children, linking their inner and outer worlds. The experience is a transformation milestone for the children. They realise that their inner worlds can be successfully converted into writing. When this is shared and recognised by friends the true power and joy of writing is experienced. It is vital we do not underestimate the significance of these entries for children as developing writers; the phrases and words, whether written in isolation or as labels, notes or commentaries to the reader, are being written into their memories.

Writing journals provided the vehicle for children's "own language" writing. I realised that when children were given personal choice about what to write they made connections between their inner and outer worlds. They wrote about the worlds of home and family, school, friends and about music, television, films, magazines, radio, internet and videos.

Children used writing journals to achieve a transformation of their inner and outer worlds – their personal space, and they did so via a literacy path. They made links between the rhythms of their spoken language and the text. The most powerful time was when they shared their journals with others in the classroom. It was then that the classroom truly became a cor unity of readers, writers and creative individuals.

Placing yourself within the text
During this writing transformation stage, children are undertaking a process of writing themselves into the text. Readers learn to hear the rhythm and cadence of different texts; they also learn to make connections between their

own world and the world described within the story. Readers do this at all levels, from early childhood into old age: they identify with the story being told and, when personal identification is strong and the reader "clicks" with the characters and situations being described, they start to place themselves within the text. Personal identification can become so absorbing that a reader even begins to speak in the style of a favourite character.

This is a natural stage in learning language. Children are receptive to this transformation and assimilation of their different inner and outer worlds. Nasser (Y6), a child dominated by his peers in class, wanted to become as powerful as the world wrestling champion Rock in his writing journal:

"So you think yer so tall and big. Well, let me tell you something, you can have a whole family reunion, you can bring them all here, because time after time, minute after minute the Rock is gonna lay you down."

Children soak up the daily input from their unique environments of home, school, peers and media; they refine and define their surroundings to create a language that is unique and evolving: their own literacy cultural capital (Bourdieu 1977). Permission to write this language of personal culture is an essential stage in the development of the child's written voice and the ultimate production of confident young writers.

Writing journals allow children to do this. The journals are full of writing and pictures about popular culture: favourite sayings and playground chants, personalised tags and secret symbols, songs and factfiles. Lisa (Y6) writes the words of a popular song, organising different verses for her friends to sing:

"Shreena's Bit: I got 21 seconds to pass my mind, I got 21 seconds to say what I have to say, But you don't like me anyway, So I won't hesitate..."

Another area of journal writing is about the home: anecdotes of family occasions, photographs of family, pets, friends, birthdays, weddings, religious festivals and holidays. Uma rates Bollywood actors in factfiles:

"One of my favourite films is called Kabhi Khashi Kabhi Ghum, songs in the film include Shavah Shavah Maheya and Deevana Deevana."

Children also write about the community and culture of their classroom: peer-group, school environment and teachers. They do surveys, quizzes and questionnaires, all encouraging the sharing of ideas and viewpoints and cementing the identity and self-esteem of the child within school context. Adam writes a moving letter to a pretend neighbour after hearing about the death of a teacher's husband:

"I am writing to tell you how sorry I am about your wife, I know how it feels. If you don't mind I'm coming over on Monday and I'll bring some ginger biscuits too. This might make it worst but, well, everyone has to die one time. I'm so sorry, hope your OK."

By assimilating different experiences, children make real and literate sense of their constantly developing place in the world.

I began to think of a name to best describe the type of writing the children produce during the free choice of writing journals. It may be referred to as *"twenty-first century style of literacy,"* as the illustrations, style and layout of text is rated highly by the children (Bearne and Kress, 2001). It may be referred to as a *"hybrid text"* (Dyson 1997), as the writing is a combination of the worlds of both home and school. My own description is the *"genre of the child"*, since this acknowledges the age of young writers. The present emphasis of children writing in the style of adults means that this is an area forgotten in literacy education.

Chapter 3
ORGANISING WRITING JOURNAL SESSIONS
Lynda Graham

Following the success of writing journals in Annette's Y6 class, we invited experienced teacher-researchers to join a writing project with the specific aim of introducing writing journals into a range of primary classrooms. Throughout the year these teachers met regularly to discuss their work and talk about ways of managing writing journal sessions. Discussion was central to the success of the project. Together, teachers forged common understandings about ways of working.

At the beginning of the year Annette explained how she introduced journals to her class by discussing ideas for possible journal entries and establishing guidelines for ways of working. All teachers adopted this approach (Graham 2003). However, as writing journals became established, children began to test these boundaries. When this happened teachers stopped the session and, with the children, re-established the ground-rules. Although children were given a great deal of autonomy in writing journal sessions, teachers expected children to use their time wisely.

All teachers invited children to cover their journals. Children took great pride in this, decorating covers with images from their own lives and worlds outside school. The journals looked very different from other exercise books and were already a bridge between the worlds of home and of school, the covers themselves an example of children bringing their own worlds into the classroom.

Towards the end of the Writing Journal Project, I visited journal sessions in each of the eleven classes. From Reception to Y6, there was a cry of *"YES!!"* when the teacher said it was writing journal time. Children themselves decided where to sit, organised resources, and began work with very little visible guidance from the teacher. They were clearly eager to begin. Many browsed first, some shared earlier entries with friends. Within minutes children were absorbed, and this continued as they wrote, drew and shared their journal entries. How had teachers created this impressive working environment?

As the project progressed teachers developed common understandings about managing writing journal sessions. Teachers thought hard about their own role. From the beginning, children produced high-quality work, but Vivienne Esparon (Y5) voiced the concerns of many when she said *"I wander around, pretty free, still feeling guilty, should I be doing some sort of instruction?"* Annette told us how she had deliberately stopped herself saying things like *"comma there... wasted space!... who told you to cut that picture up?..."* She realised that the teaching interventions we make during the rest of the school day are not appropriate in writing journal sessions. Teachers wanted to give children a sense of independence and autonomy about the quality of their journal entries. The extent to which children took this responsibility very seriously, producing work of a high standard, is described in chapter 5. Children re-worked some entries and abandoned others. They took responsibility for their work. Kim Lawrence (Y5) spoke for many in the project when she stated *"I'm luxuriating...I'm so needed at other times"*.

We discovered that the teaching role is different in writing journal sessions. The teachers:

• *...made informal observations of the children*

At the beginning of each session, teachers watched to check that children were not being left out. Some children opt to work alone: for instance, during my visit, a Y6 boy in Linda Callaghan's class was writing alone about fishing, itself a solitary activity. However, many children prized the social aspect of writing journal sessions, and teachers intervened sensitively if they thought a child was being left out. Kim Lawrence told me, *"I'm looking for the lost and lonely"*.

During each session teachers used time to observe their children as writers. Pat Parlour (Y4) explained, *"I often stand back and watch one person, observing how he or she manages their writing"*. Sarah Hayward (Y1/2) realised that *"getting to know so much about the children"* through these observations, was central to teachers' developing knowledge and understanding about the children as writers.

• *...responded to invitations to share on-going work*

Children often invited their teacher to share work during the session. Teachers took journal entries seriously, and engaged in genuine conversation about the work. Annette spoke for us all when she stated *"I seem to be responding as*

Annette not Ms Johnson'. Clearly, teachers themselves enjoy the sessions as much as the children. Gaynor Talley (Y2) confirmed this when she told me, *"what an enjoyable and relaxing oasis journal time is, away from the stresses of having to fit everything else in"*

• *...arranged sharing times at the end of each session*
Teachers invited children to read their work to the class at the end of every session. This sharing was vital. Barrs and Cork (2001) call it *'public reading'* and found reading aloud to be of greater value to young writers than traditional displays of finished writing. Young authors needed opportunities to hear their work read aloud to an audience in order to experience to effect of their writing on others. Children in the Writing Journal Project knew that the sharing sessions are valuable; Jack (Y5) told me: *"Of course you need to share at the end, it's how you get ideas"*.

• *...established and maintained a writing journal community*
The participatory presence of the class teacher is central to the success of writing journals. This became very clear as Christmas loomed. Project teachers were often involved in rehearsals and supply teachers, who had not previously been involved in the writing journal community, took over the journal sessions. Sometimes ways of working were changed, and plenaries were often missed. Children began to take less care and journal entries lost vigour and became scrappy. We realised that the discreet management of the class teacher was crucial to the success of writing journals. She was a central part of the writing journal community. Without her, writing journal sessions disintegrated.

Writing Journals in the Reception class...
Carol Domingo, the Reception teacher, adapted Annette's framework by inviting children to draw, not write, in their journals. Each journal session began with a story read aloud. Children were then invited to draw this story, or choose their own focus. Influenced by the work of Carol Fox (Fox 1993), Carol Domingo found a way of bringing children's oral storytelling skills into the classroom by scribing the stories the children created from their illustrations, covering every child over two or three sessions.

What did the children do?

During writing journal sessions children are given a great deal of autonomy. How did they respond to this? The children:

- *...choose what to write*

This was a huge incentive. Formerly reluctant writers revelled in the opportunity to write about what really mattered to them.

- *...choose where to work, and who with*

Independence is crucial in developing a community of fellow enthusiasts. We knew from the Croydon Reading Project (Graham, 1999) that boys needed to work with other boys to develop a community of readers. The same is true for writing journals. Children needed a free choice, and this often meant that they chose to work in gender groups. In Linda O'Callaghan's Y6 class a group of ten boys moved tables so that they could all be together. Only two boys worked collaboratively. All the others worked on individual pieces of work, but read aloud on-going work to each other, and offered much appreciated praise and encouragement.

- *...moved around the classroom*

Gardner (1993) reminds us that people have *'multiple intelligences'*. Kinaesthetic learners need movement. Many adults (including me) need to move away from the computer during the writing process in order to think. Many also need to share on-going work with friends and colleagues. The freedom to move in writing journal sessions and to share on-going work with fellow enthusiasts, gave children an opportunity to work within preferred styles of learning. In Pat Parlour's Y4 class, a group of boys worked standing round a table. In Sarah Hayward's Y1/2 and Joanne Greenhalgh's Y3 class a number of children chose to work sitting and lying on the floor.

- *...talked with others*

Vygotsky (1978) realised that thought is not only expressed in words, but that it comes into existence through words. Children used writing journal sessions to think their thoughts aloud. They talked their journal entries into existence, and read and sang entries aloud as they work. They used talk to share and to trade resources and to seek feedback and advice. Children encouraged, praised, and laughed with each other as they worked.

- *...shared with other children*

Many children used their journals to create social networks through their writing. They included each other in the lists, stories and games they created, and used quiz and survey genres to forge links with each other in the classroom. For instance, one shy Y6 boy commented *'I'm getting real respect today...usually people don't talk to me, but they want to answer my survey about computer games'.*

- *...chose to write as experts*

We knew from other projects that children needed opportunities to write as experts (Graham 2001). Writing journals gave children this opportunity. In writing journals children demonstrated their existing knowledge and understanding about the craft of writing and the worlds of home, school and popular culture.

- *... worked at their own pace*

Children took time over journal entries and re-visited favourite themes. Carol Domingo (Reception) realised that this is important, commenting, *"...just as children choose the same book again and again, in writing journals they have been able to re-visit themes, and have felt the need to do so."*

- *...revised and re-worked journal entries*

Children also revised and re-worked journal entries. Harry (Y1) chose to write about his two gerbils. He typed his entry on the computer, stuck it in his journal and shared the writing with the class. Two months later his teacher, Sarah Haward, noticed him revising his original entry. One of the gerbils had died and this event was clearly significant to Harry. He did not choose to read his revised version to the class, but wanted an accurate record in his writing journal. The amended version (see Fig 3.1) is a remarkable piece of grammatical self-editing, and illustrates the importance of writing journals to the children themselves.

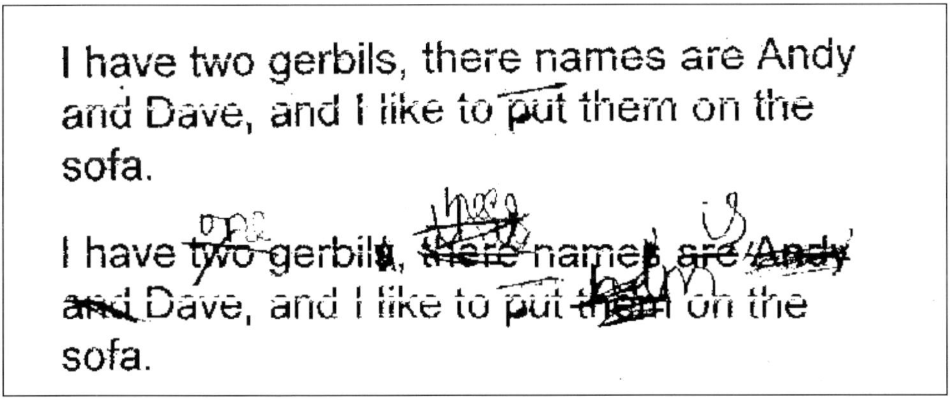

I have two gerbils, there names are Andy and Dave, and I like to put them on the sofa.

I have two gerbils, there names are Andy and Dave, and I like to put them on the sofa.

Fig. 3.1: Harry's original and re-worked journal entries

Mutual trust and respect

In every class there was a relationship of mutual trust and respect between teacher and pupils, and between the pupils themselves. This relationship had been central to children's development as readers in the Croydon KS2 Reading Project (Graham 1999), central to their development as writers, and crucial in writing journal sessions. One example from Y1 demonstrates this. The class teacher, Irene Napier, was unwell, and a supply teacher took the writing journal session. Simon kept his entry secret and did not want to share it with anyone but was eager to show it to Irene, and the rest of the class, when she returned. He had wanted his teacher to be the first to know...*'I can do back flips'* (see Fig 3.2)

Fig.3.2: I can do back-flips

Chapter 4
SHOULD I LET THEM DRAW?
Annette Johnson

Without doubt, the main worry that teachers mention concerns the children's need for illustrations in their writing journals. Although the concept of visual literacy is accepted and children are surrounded by - even bombarded with - illustrated messages, there is a 'knee jerk' reaction against allowing children to draw in their books. Yet the drawings children include in their journals are the visual counterpart to the written choices they are making.

We encourage the use of quality picture books to convey meaning in a story and drawing is recognised as a natural developmental stage for young children in their journey to become literate. However, opportunities to draw in school diminish as children get older. A storyboard narrative activity in Year 1 is considered good literacy development; the same use of illustration in Year 6 will need to be justified. A teacher who limits drawing in the early years would be questioned, 'Where are the opportunities for meaning-making in the learning environment?' Yet older children's meaning-making and visual literacy through personal illustration also needs support. When children draw in their writing journals they are fulfilling a desire to reproduce symbolic representations of their ideas.

The National Curriculum in Art (DfEE 1999) ensures that children experience a variety of artistic genres and reproduce their own illustrations within each. Art lessons are no longer opportunities to draw and paint in their own styles but times to discuss other artists' work. As in literacy, personal choice is limited. Writing journals allow children to work on, and develop, their personal artistic style.

The inclusion of well-known paintings - even film "shorts" - is now recommended elements for a creative and innovative literacy hour. If the use of visual imagery is an acceptable aid for text comprehension, the need for children to draw during the process of communication should be viewed as a natural and logical response. Disapproval of children drawing is effectively stunting their literacy process; it denies them a natural choice in attributing meaning to language. Stephen's picture of a digger was drawn during the foot and mouth crisis (see Fig 4.1). His drawing perfectly captures the images seen daily in the media at that time and, as Stephen's relatives are farmers, it also conveys his personal interest.

Fig 4.1: Stephen's digger

Writing journals let children draw in a style they choose, about subjects of personal interest and to reproduce symbols and patterns from their everyday surroundings and personal culture. Within their illustrations, children combine personal and communal experiences into new transformations that have a unique personal interest and relevance; through this process they learn to make meaning and thus make sense of their environment.

Charlotte's picture of an alien hand (see Fig 4.2) is such a transformation, produced from several previous journal entries and illustrations. The hand outline originally circulated around the class during Divali, when many children created their own Mendhi patterns; the long claws and hairs match the front cover of a horror book read by Charlotte and the example of scaly skin was influenced by a class journal craze of creating colourful patterns using squared paper. Finally Charlotte added the webbed fingers, the title Asrai Hand and caption "Sadly this species is now extinct". In creating this illustration Charlotte had been influenced by the reading of a former SAT comprehension story: a fable about the Asrai, a mythical species that lived underwater. Charlotte had linked this literacy hour text, the shared experience of drawing Mendhi patterns, the class journal craze for geometric patterns and the cover illustration of a class book. In producing this drawing she had given visual and literacy meaning to a text whose story had interested and "clicked" with her.

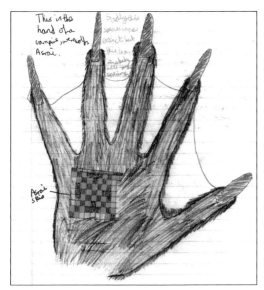

Fig 4.2: Charlotte's Asrai Hand

Charlotte's picture and caption are an example of a child's illustrated genre which can be easily over-looked or dismissed as an elaborate doodle with no connection to literacy development. In reality the hand of the Asrai is the symbolic centre of the fable; when it grips a human it leaves a burning mark upon the individual as a warning and constant reminder of the human's selfish behaviour. By choosing to draw the Asrai hand Charlotte focused on the climactic scene and the moral comment within this traditional tale. Her illustration showed comprehension of the moral message and a literacy deduction that is both accurate and succinct.

For children, illustration is a natural expression of their literacy, a means to communicate and transform their ideas and insights. It is teachers and adults who need to re-learn the skills of visual literacy and encourage its use in meaning-making, inference and deduction.

Chapter 5
WRITING LIKE WRITERS
Lynda Graham

Writing journals give children an opportunity to write like writers. In understanding how writers write it may be useful to think first about how readers read.

Creating readers and writers

Readers make time to read. They read for fun, for information, and to explore what matters to them in inner and outer worlds. Readers choose to read, and choose what to read. For instance, Joel, aged two and a half, chooses to read several times a day, sometimes on his own, often with an adult. He loves funny lines like *'stinky old Dad'* (Rosen 2001), and memorable phrases like *'Hairy Maclary from Donaldson's Dairy'* (Dodd 1985). He reads and re-reads scary books like *'Knock Knock who's there?'* (Grindley 1995), and studies the BRIO catalogue looking for additions to his train set. Joel chooses books he has heard read by others – he chooses to abandon some books and spend time with others, reading, re-reading and talking about them with adults. He is a reader. The diagram (Fig.5.1) represents Joel's readerly behaviour. It applies to readers young and old.

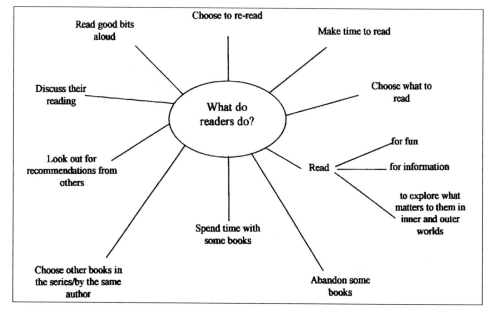

Fig.5.1: Joel's behaviour as a reader

Joel is fortunate. His family love spending time reading to him, and have introduced him to many books. Because of this good 'teaching', Joel has become a reader.

The project teachers realised that, before using writing journals, they were teaching writing but not giving children the opportunity to become writers. Writers choose to write, and choose what to write. They write for fun, to share information, and to explore what matters to them in their inner and outer worlds. They choose to work on some pieces of writing and to abandon others. They are influenced by other writers, and discuss their writing with those they trust. The teachers realised that few of the behaviours in Fig 5.1 were developed by their writing curriculum. Writing journals are important because they give children time in the busy school day to become writers. The following case-studies show how children responded to this.

Joanne, Reception
Children in Carol Domingo's Reception class drew in their journals, and dictated stories from these pictures. We were to find that this was important for assured as well as beginner writers. Joanne spent time on her illustrations, and her dictated stories are descriptions of her drawings. An early picture of a little old lady holding a cat's lead reads:
> *"One day a little lady was walking out with her cat. When she talked to her cat, her cat said 'My name is called Tiggin'. The princess was happy to have a talking cat, but she didn't tell anyone because it was a secret."*

Joanne developed her story by talking aloud to the picture. Princesses and animals were recurring themes throughout her journal. In the same way that writers return to favourite subjects and themes, Joanne re-worked her illustration, of a character holding the lead of an animal during the year. A summer entry is of a young girl with a crown, holding the lead of a cat. The layout is remarkably similar to earlier illustrations but, this time two birds are flying in the sky, together with one covered in spots apparently falling. Her dictated story reads:
> *"One day there was a little girl walking out with her pussy cat and she saw two birds up in the sky. She looked down on the ground to her cat, then she saw a dead bird. She picked it up, only a tiny bit with two fingers like this, and she looked on it and there was 100 ants on it. She dropped it."*

Carol noted that Joanne also used her journal to draw pictures of friends and family and to *'reflect and refashion experiences in her life'*, as she made her illustrations. Asked at the end of the year to choose her favourite pages she chose one about Christmas and two about birthday parties. Joanne was not particularly interested in the dictated words, instead *'...it was the memory of the real thing which excited her'*. However, Joanne's final choice was of the recurring theme of a character holding a lead. Again the person is a little girl with a lead, though this time the animal is a rat. She chose the page because she liked the rat and rainbow in the picture (see fig.5.2). For the first time she remembered part of her dictated story.

It begins:

> *"The princess is out in the middle of the street, under the sky, under the sun, under the rainbow".*

She repeated the poetic dictation of the opening in exactly the same sing-song voice used when she had shared it with the class. She had invented her written text as she made her illustration, and internalised her own chanted speech pattern. Not only was she using drawing to symbolise meaning (Barrs 1988a p51-69), she was also beginning to tune into rhythms of written language.

Fig. 5.2: Girl with a lead and a rat

Hassan, Reception

At the beginning of the year Hassan already had a small written sight vocabulary, and could use initial, end and medial sounds in his writing, though the teacher noted that he was *'inhibited by anxiety about spelling'* and did not choose to write. He too revelled in the opportunity to draw in his journal. All Hassan's stories were about imagined worlds inspired by film, TV and computer games. His favourite dictated story reads:

> *"The Power Rangers saw the baddies. They fighted them. They crashed them with their swords. They beat them and they got treasure which was hidden in the baddies base. The baddies base didn't have any shields on it. They bought lots of morphers with the money."*

The words describe the fast-moving action of a scene from a text in his head. He chose the journal entry, like Joanne, for the details in his illustration. He particularly liked his depiction of the lead Power Ranger:

See- he's the only one who's got the long swords, the others have just got ordinary swords'. (see Fig 5.3)

Fig. 5.3: Hassan's Power Ranger

Although Hassan did not chose to write about friends, friendship was at the heart of his journal work. Carol wrote: "*Power Rangers have great meaning for three boys in the class. Hassan and another boy are both sparring to be 'best friend' of the third, who has the most Power Ranger toys. It sometimes seems that liking Power Rangers is connected with perceived worthiness to be 'best friend'. The boys watch videos at each other's houses, play with the toys and read the comics. Power Rangers consolidate their friendship*". Like readers who choose to read and writers who choose to write, he returned to favourite themes in his journal. Carol noticed these were themes which "*reasserted his 'boyishness' and confirmed and consolidated his position in the group*".

Making stories from multi-modal texts is a challenging task (Bearne 2002). Hassan coped by focusing on one scene, capturing the image in a detailed drawing, and describing the action and movement in words. By the end of the year Hassan was a fluent reader. He spelt many words accurately, consistently used letter strings and an adult could read his writing easily. However, in looking overall at his writing during the year, he chose his Power Ranger and Action

Man illustrations as favourites. Although he was able to represent the world symbolically in writing, he treasured ways in which he could do so through image.

Tim, Year 1

Tim was an inexperienced writer at the beginning of the project, still at a very early stage of understanding how language is written down, and he didn't usually like to write. However his teacher, Irene Napier, noticed that he loved writing in his writing journal. He sat with a group of boys and wrote a series of entries about Thunderbirds. For the first time his writing was recognisable. One entry, boldly illustrated, read

"this is Thunderbird 1 when it's ready to blast off" (revised spelling).

He chose this entry as a favourite, commenting that the drawing of the Thunderbird was easy *"because it's an easy shape"*. What was difficult was *"getting the bs and ds the right way round"*. Other favourite entries in the first few months included one about liking golf *"...because I'm going to play golf with my granddad"* and one about the Air Force *"...because when I go to Tenerife I'm going to go on a plane and I like flying"*.

Fig. 5.4: "I have ejected"

Tim used his journal to capture fond memories and explore enthusiasms. He wrote 'TB5', talked about this, and then wrote *"I haf ejektid"* in a speech bubble (see Fig 5.4). He was delighted with this and asked to read it out in the plenary. When his teacher gave him Thunderbird stickers, he wrote eagerly, evidencing *"a strength of hand control never before seen"*. He worked with a group of boys, and could be heard telling one, stuck for a word: *'Just do what you hear'*. In writing as an expert about Thunderbirds, Tim developed confidence in his writing, and began to make progress as a writer, moving on from Level 1-2 on the CLPE Writing Scale 1.

Susie, Year 1

Susie also progressed significantly as a writer during the project year. At the beginning her teacher noted that she was *'really focussed'* in her writing journal work, *'writing copiously'* with *'real conviction and interest'*. She wrote about her life in and out of school, her outings, her friends and her family; she wrote about her world. Like many of her friends in the class, she was concerned about the presentation of her work, and chose favourite pieces, for the presentation as well as the fond memories they elicited.

Fig 5.5: Susie's coloured-in writing

She started a class presentation craze of colouring-in the centre parts of all lower case letters. Her all-time favourite journal piece was like this, a beautifully presented page which reads *"I love my teddy and my mummy and DaDDy and my dog and my cat"* (see Fig 5.5). Susie commented: *"The writing was easy because I know how to spell all those words. The hard bit was drawing the hairs on the teddy"*.

Like many others, she delighted in celebrating words she knew and wrote about things she liked and loved. Her texts were treasured and decorated, in the same way that early monks decorated their sacred texts. Susie returned over and over again to the theme of 'like' and 'love' as she celebrated her newly acquired skills. She was learning, implicitly, that writing is *'the representation of meaning by symbolic signs'* (Vygotsky 1978). By the end of the year she completed whole sides of A4, with beautifully decorated repeated statements like: *"I love mummy and she loves me, I love my teacher and she loves me, I love my dog and he loves me…"*.

Susie became increasingly confident as a writer, and made very real progress, moving from level 2 to 4 on the CLPE Writing Scale 1 (Barrs, ibid).

Jordan, Year 2

Unlike Susie, Jordan did not at first write with enthusiasm. His early journal entries were copied story beginnings. The entries were scrappy, and some unfinished. Over time his handwriting became gradually more legible and he began to use cursive script. His first original entry was a drawing of an imaginary, smiling monster captioned *'it can jump'*.

More abandoned copied stories were followed by a dramatic whole page cut-out picture of a wrestler riding a motorbike. Jordan then began to work with a group of boys cutting and sticking pictures from a Lego magazine. This activity seemed to draw a small group of boys together in friendship (Marsh & Millard, 2000). Jordan's first Lego entry was accompanied by a diagram and list of instructions for a race:

> *"pull back motor 5…pull back motor 4…pull back motor 1…"*

Jordan's second journal began confi-dently with several copied stories and more Lego pictures, increasingly accompanied by written commentaries. He then invented a monster called a *"Foo foo FBI kit"*. It is a hybrid text

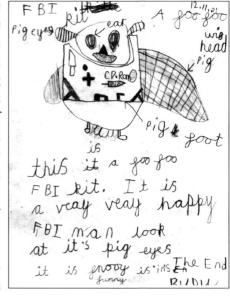

Fig. 5.6: Jordan's favourite entry, his Foo Foo FBI Kit

(Dyson 1997) melding ideas from *'Little Rabbit Foo Foo'* (Rosen 1999) and the FBI from television. The detailed drawing is labelled. He wrote: *"this is a foo foo FBI kit. It is a veay veay happy FBI man look at it's pig eyes it is fnooy (funny)"*. (see Fig. 5.6) This was Jordan's favourite entry *"because I like the funny name and I made it up myself"*. He had begun to find his voice as a writer. Both drawing and handwriting ooze confidence. He is a *'twenty-first century literacy maker'* (Graham & Johnson 2002) using words and illustration to create his own original text.

Tucked away between these pages are signs of an important developing friendship: *'James likes me you know…James is a bee who looks like a monster'*. Towards the end of the project Jordan, and other boys in the friendship group began to copy poems. One of the Jordan's final entries is an original poem; it reads:*'One night I had a fright It was a light in sight. By James and Jordan'*. Jordan loved being able to sit with other boys of his own choice and, through a common interest in Legoland catalogues, the boys developed strong friend-ships. This was important to Jordan in his developing confidence as a writer. He made good progress, moving on from 3-4 on the CLPE Writing Scale 1.

Massimo, Year 3
Massimo, in Joanne Greenhalgh's Y3 class, also became a social writer. He said: *"I like doing writing journals because you can sit with a friend"*. One of his first journal entries was a series of beautifully drawn comic portraits of his *"friendship gang"*, with himself as *'The master'*. (see front cover)

In Y4 he chose his favourite Y3 entries. He liked a long skeleton story, saying: *"I couldn't sleep, and wanted to make up a story. I read it to the class, they liked it, and so I carried on for six chapters"*. Massimo talked about the importance of the class as audience for his work, but also used his journal to forge friendships. The skeleton story, like many others, reflects the importance of friendship, featuring the gang and their teacher on a scary camping holiday.

Design and illustration were also central to Massimo's journal entries. He created a series of 'WANTED' animal posters, using 'smudge pencil' techniques he had learnt from a television programme. He was delighted to re-discover his comic illustration *"The World's strongest insect"*, saying *"I wanted to make the class laugh"*. During the year he received a much coveted Game

Boy as a present, drew it from every angle and then used a cut out illustration from a magazine saying *"Matthew let me cut up the game cube as I couldn't copy the controller".*

Massimo's Y3 journal ends with a series of beautifully presented jokes; a snake information booklet; and a complicated 'War Race' board game. This board game is an example of a symbolic 'Map of Play' described by Barrs (1988b). He explained: *"...the friends race all kinds of cars, it's a race with war in it, if they're damaged they go to the garage...it takes weeks...there is a big eye ball with eye balls coming out of it..."* Just as children need to symbolise their thinking through drawing, we found that many, like Massimo, also invented maps of play in their journals.

The craze for writing about snakes had started several months earlier with an impressive series of entries from a fellow gang member who was saving-up for his own snake. By Y4 he had achieved his aim, and several children, like Massimo, were also writing about snakes. In his new Y4 journal Massimo developed this snake theme, drawing the gang again, naming them *'The Club Snake'.* All the club members had nicknames, with Massimo as the *'Desert King Snake'.* The special club rule was *'We will always be friends'.* Dyson described a classroom in which young authors engage in *'social fun'* (Dyson 1997 p35) as they chose friends to rehearse and act out the stories they have written. Like the children in Dyson's study, Massimo's major concern was not learning to write, but he used writing *'as a tool for social learning'.* Through this, he made marked progress in writing during the project year, moving from 5-6 on the CLPE Writing Scale 1. He also became a writer, using writing to explore his own world and his own imagined world.

Himani, Year 5
Himani also used her writing journal to explore her own world in the company of friends. Like Jordan, she was conscious of improvements in her handwriting: *"Before my handwriting was not nice and was not joined, and now is as all nice and joined".*

She began by working in companionship with two other girls. Slightly different versions of her early entries: a story of a walking robot, a poem about the deep blue sea, and cut out pictures of East Enders and Harry Potter also appear in her friends' journals. Himani drew pictures of the friendship group, and then wrote a long list of her favourite Hindu films. A story about a bully followed, slightly different versions appearing in her friends' journals. Next, all three girls stuck a picture of a Bollywood film into their journals, each writing *"...it's all about loving your parents"* under their pictures.

Then the girls began to work collaboratively, composing a play-script, which they later performed to the class. It was entitled *'Mohobbetein'*, and Himani wrote: *'Why? It's called this because it means love, and we are doing a play about love'*. All three girls wrote identical, beautifully presented copies of the script in their journals. They then went on to create a Bollywood film script which was also performed (see Fig 5.7). Himani explained the theme in her journal: *'Whenever you want to achieve something, think of your parents and watch, you will win'*.

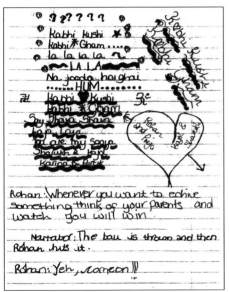

Fig. 5.7: Himani's Bollywood film script

Himani and her friends made marked progress during the year, Himani moving on from 3-4 on CLPE Writing Scale 2 (Barrs ibid). The girls brought their own worlds into the classroom, first the worlds of East Enders and Harry Potter, and then that of Bollywood films. The scripts were written with great care, and Kim Lawrence, their teacher, noticed them rehearsing in playtimes ready for performances to the class. Through their writing journals the three girls explored their *'...own ways of seeing and understanding and representing the world to themselves'* (Brooker 2002 p.171). Bernstein realised that this sharing of worlds was central to the child's learning. *'If the culture of the teacher is to become part of the consciousness of the child, then the culture of the child must first be in the consciousness of the teacher'* (Bernstein 1970 p.31). Kim Lawrence welcomed children's own worlds in the classroom, and noted the girls' growing confidence and independence. Himani herself realised that *'..as well as having fun we get to learn. Whilst you're having fun you don't even know that you're learning'*.

Tyronne, Year 5

In Vivienne Esparon's class, Tyronne also moved from 3-4 on the CLPE Writing Scale 2. He felt that *"journals are fun because you get to do your stuff in your own time. Sometimes work can get boring. In journals you can just relax and write… you're allowed to sit where you want, to talk to friends and write what you feel"*. Tyronne chose to take his journal home to spend additional time on it.

His journal began with an introduction to himself, his family, friends and hobbies. He revisited these themes throughout his journal, writing about incidents in family life, favourite television programmes, computer games, CDs, films, books, wrestling and football. He wrote about his life. Occasionally he worked at illustrations, and talked aloud to his journal as he did so: *"I know you already know that I'm crazy about Dragon Ball Z but I've never drawn one so I'm going to have a go"*.

His favourite journal entry was about football information: *"I like football and I like information, and it looks colourful. I cut the badges out of a football book, and that was difficult because I'm not good at cutting. The writing was easy, it was just collecting information. My*

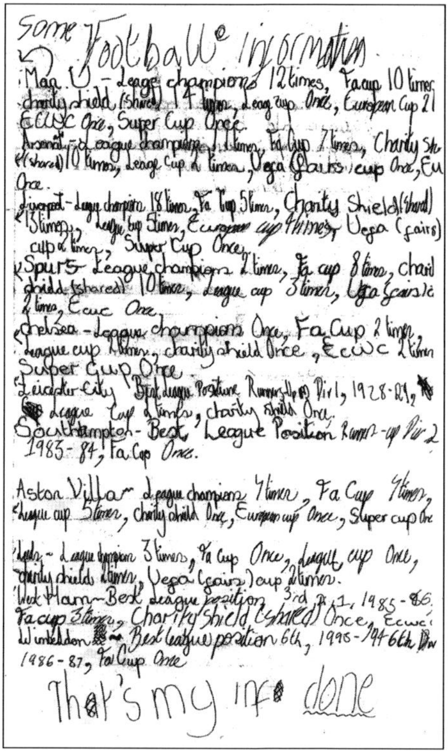

Fig 5.8: Information about football teams

favourite part was writing about Manchester United, they're my favourite team. Also, it's the first time I used the gel pens". (see fig. 5.8).

This mattered to Tyrone. He spent several days working on it, taking great care with the presentation, and battling with his cutting out skills. He was still proud of it at the end of the project saying, *"I like to look back because I can find information I need. It looks colourful and I was proud of myself when I'd done it"*.

Lucy, Year 6

Lucy in Jenny Llewellyn's Y6 class, was already an experienced writer. In the first term she wrote: a story called 'Mum'; a Halloween curse; a letter in the first person written as a memorial to passengers on flight 667; a play; three poems; information about herself; a diagram about the perfect parent (see back cover); an abandoned story; a letter to J.K.Rowling; a story about pixies; and a Victorian diary written in the first person.

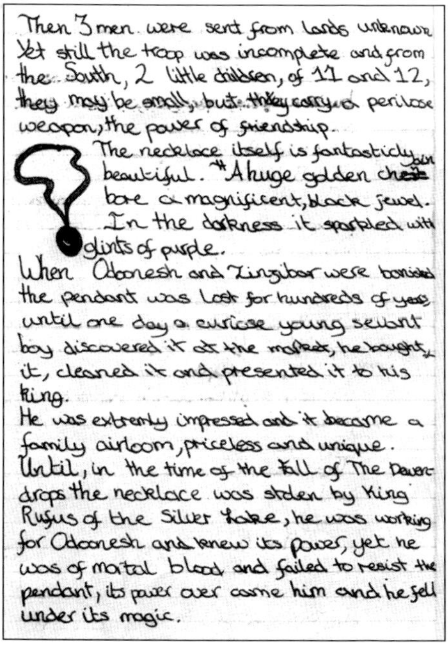

Then 3 men were sent from lands unknown
Yet still the troop was incomplete and from
the South, 2 little children, of 11 and 12,
they may be small, but they carry a perilose
weapon, the power of friendship.
The necklace itself is fantasticly
beautiful. *A huge golden chest
bore a magnificent, black jewel.
In the darkness it sparkled with
glints of purple.
When Odooresh and Zingibar were banised
the pendant was lost for hundreds of years
until one day a curious young servant
boy discovered it at the market, he bought
it, cleaned it and presented it to his
king.
He was extremly impressed and it became a
family airloom, priceless and unique.
Until, in the time of the fall of The Power
drops the necklace was stolen by King
Rufus of the Silver take, he was working
for Odooresh and knew its power, yet he
was of mortal blood and failed to resist the
pendant, its power over came him and he fell
under its magic.

Fig 5.9: Part of Lucy's chapter story

She began term two by spending several days writing a list of unusual names, 320 altogether. After an abandoned start of a film script for the Hobbit, Lucy began a story, which she later re-titled 'the Enchanted Pendant'. This story was sustained over a period of four months. Long chapters of five or six pages were re-read and revised over time. Each section ended with the words *'to be continued'*. (see Fig 5.9) Interspersed, as Lucy mulled over ideas, were: profiles of friends; clapping games; songs; netball moves; risqué poems about teachers, friends and family; and an abandoned start to a new story. By the end of the project Lucy said that her favourite writing in the whole year was *'most definitely my writing in my writing journal…I have learned to plan over time'*. By the end of the project she was an exceptionally experienced writer, moving on from level 4-5 on CLPE Writing Scale 2.

Adam, Y6

Adam found his voice as a writer through his writing journal. At the end of the project he thought about his school journey of learning to write, and wrote: *"I felt sad at times with my writing but now I feel...great (as you can see) because now I use joined up writing. Before I used to be scared of it, I thought it would be messy"*.

Certainly his handwriting changed from script to a confident cursive style in his journal. When asked how he would feel if writing journals were banned, he said: *"I would feel down because I find writing journals a multi-choice, you can write what you feel"*.

Adam covered his journal with pictures of wrestlers, but these did not feature inside. His first page was a brief introduction to himself, including his favourite food. He then wrote three nonsense poems, taking great delight in making them funny, and in playing with rhyme and alliteration. On Friday 13th, he wrote a piece: *'Is Friday 13th the worst day of your life?'*, with references to Adam and Eve, Cain and Abel, and Jesus. These became the themes of his journal: food; religion; humorous, slightly subversive writing; joy in the sound of words. For instance, an early shopping list includes : *"turtle burger, bloodade, cheese oil, washing up noodle"*, and a poem, the line: *"Last week I found out David Beckham came from Peckham"*.

A story *'Three little ants and the Big Bad Human'* was his first sustained entry. Jenny Llewellyn wrote: *'This story marked the start of his popularity in school as a story teller.'* He read it to the class and to other classes in the school, giving *'public readings'* for his work (Barrs and Cork 2001 p.213). Adam experienced how others responded warmly to his humour, and his delight in wordplay. He told his teacher:
"I take an idea and twist it a bit to make it my own idea".

The story begins:
> *"Once in a little shed floor lived three little ants named Pop and Crop and Little Bop. 'We need to find a new house', stuffing his mouth with maggot flakes said Bop"*.

The ants found a new house in a coke can. Suddenly, a human

"'shuffled his foot in the mud 'Get out of the can you ants or I'll crush and mush and break your house down'.
'Not by the antennae of my ting ting ting!' squeaked the ants.
'So the human crashed and he mushed and he broke the can down.'"

Adam wrote several more short stories. A rhythmic poem about pizza and lemonade, was followed by a piece written just before Christmas:

Ok Andrew, nice and clearly, off you go
Welcome everybody to our school concert

Louder, please. Andrew. Mums and dads won't hear you at the back will they
Welcome everybody to our school concert

Louder, Andrew. You're not trying
Pro-ject-your-voice.
Take a big breath and louder.
Welcome everybody to our school concert

Now, Andrew, there is no need to be silly

Adam is an oral learner. He used the sounds and rhythms from written texts and, as this example shows, tuned into the speech patterns around him- in this instance a fraught Christmas rehearsal. After several more humorous stories and poems, Adam returned to his earlier religious theme, and wrote a conversation between Jesus and the Devil, and then the script of a talk show in which *'Anty Dan'* interviewed Jesus. Adam moved from 3-4 on the CLPE Writing Scale 2. The journal gave him the opportunity to delight in the sound and rhythms of words, and to become a writer.

Conclusion
Children in the project wrote like writers in their journals. They chose to return to favourite themes, to abandon some writing and to spend concentrated time on other pieces. They wrote for fun, for information, and to explore what mattered to them in inner and outer worlds. They discussed ideas, took ideas from each other, and re-worked and revised entries.

Thirty years ago Connie and Harold Rosen wrote: *'No teacher can hope to know the particular anxieties, fears, delights, passions, curiosities and obsessions which are dominating the lives of children'.* (Rosen & Rosen 1973 p.84). Teachers in the project became privileged 'knowers' of the worlds of children. Vygototsky realised that the child's budding personality will not grow if children write only what the teacher thinks up (Vygotsky 1978). We saw children develop confidence in themselves as writers as they explored their passions and obsessions in writing.

Children also wrote from within their worlds. Hollindale discusses the particular state of being a child, and uses the term 'childness'. He discusses how children read texts for children through the eyes of children (Hollindale 1997, p.45-46). Our children also evidenced this 'childness' through text and images. Not only did they write about their lives at the beginning of the twenty-first century, but they created their texts using twenty-first century text-making techniques - colour, design, and image as well as print. Their texts reflect the texts they see around them: in communities, homes and schools, books, television, film and popular culture. The writing journal texts reflect children's worlds at the beginning of the twenty-first century.

End Piece:
BUILDING PROFESSIONAL CAPITAL
Eve Bearne

Recently, I asked a group of teachers to talk about something over the last week or so that they had <u>wanted</u> to write. You might like to consider the question yourself. The answers varied from letters of complaint, letters to local councils about development plans, a card to comfort a friend, a poem written with the class, a personal journal and a response on a daughter's reading journal pointing out to the teacher that she did, in fact, read at home! All of these were, to the writers, necessary writing. You don't need a great deal of imagination to think what these teachers considered were the <u>un</u>necessary writing activities they'd done in the previous week. The difference lay in drive, motivation and choice. Whilst teachers will, of course, gain professional satisfaction from the writing demands associated with their jobs, the feeling is not the same as getting something off your chest, or sharing thoughts and pleasures, or simply reflecting on paper. As adults we need to be able to experience the satisfactions of all kinds of writing, but if we don't have the chance to make choices about the ways we write, then we are less likely to experience 'effortful success', as Margaret Meek puts it (Meek 1999).

The journals described by Annette and Lynda are necessary writing. They are very potent examples of drive, motivation and choice. The experience of having the chance to write because you want to - to decorate, illustrate, review, rewrite – has clearly paid off, not just in the personal satisfactions and pride of the young writers, but in the more objective and comparable measures offered by the Primary Language Record Writing Scales and proof in the form of higher than expected SATs results. So there is evidence of the impact of using writing journals both in the way the writers feel about themselves and in their increased achievements.

For me, however, the most exciting part of the work has been how both children and teachers have been able to realise their authentic, personal different strengths. By 'realise' I mean two things: 'making real' and 'coming to understand'. By making their meaning real in the journals, the children – and their teachers - have come to understand what they know and can do. For the children, realising themselves has been to do with voice, described so vividly by

Annette in Chapter 2. And as Lynda points out, the teachers themselves have found their voices in their own reflections on the work. But there's also something about diversity and difference here which seems to me a key to the success of the project. One of the strong features that arose from my individual discussions with the teachers was their awareness of the diversity of the pupils. They are very used to catering for linguistic diversity and noticing gender differences. But they have become much more aware of a range of approaches to learning evident in the journals – the kinaesthetic learners who cut and stick and make their journals three dimensional; the aural learners who love to write rhymes, raps and songs; the spatial thinkers who automatically use whole page layout and design confidently; the analytic learners who like to build their knowledge up from part to whole; the social learners whose journals reflect an overwhelming importance of family and friends in learning; those who need a long gestation period to get their writing ideas going; and those who have enormous sustained determination.

The journals allowed for these kinds of general conclusions because they are a window on recurrent features of a writer's preferences. Whilst we may see children's writing develop over a period of time, they are usually writing what we have asked them to write. The journals show us children of all ages who choose for themselves to revisit or sustain ideas over very lengthy periods. They show recurrent features which may not be evident as children fulfil the requirements of regular writing. Their differences, shared interest and development can be very fruitfully observed through writing journals. Significantly, they have a chance to explore and display their wider text knowledge and this is very useful information for the teacher. The journals have allowed the children to reveal their individual likes and dislikes, personal expertise, knowledge and playful pleasures. It is clear that the project has done much the same for the teachers. Each had a different way of working, yet they shared a common purpose in 'letting go' a little, taking risks and trusting their pupils – and themselves. Where the children had to get used to the idea that they were in charge of their own writing in the journals, so did the teachers. It was a risky business. But it worked. There are some striking parallels between the children's and teachers' experiences, but there are also some interesting dualities, even, it might seem, oppositions. And there is much to learn about how the journals acted as a transformative catalyst.

The writing classrooms described in this book were communities of informal and, at times more formal, networks of readers and writers – and talkers and listeners, of course. Children worked with friends, broke off from writing to share jokes, discuss last night's television, plan what they might be doing at playtime, then resumed their personal writing. The highly individual act of writing became intensely social. The social and individual nature of the journals is one of the dualities which seems significant to me: operating within the important social network of the classroom community yet giving the chance for the children to expressing themselves as individual social beings.

The public and the private: finding and negotiating spaces

The motif of 'space' has become a feature of the project: space for the children to develop ideas, play with language, explore their own worlds as writers - making space and time for reflection. This applies equally to the project affording the teachers spaces to think. But there is also a strong aspect of 'negotiating spaces'. This might be a practical and physical matter of finding opportunities for collaboration and individual undisturbed writing, but it is also a matter of personal and social space within our thinking. The journals have allowed the rehearsal and exploration of the personal spaces in the mind and how these accommodate to the social spaces and distances of relationships with others. This is reflected in the use of the journal both as a chance for monologue and a means of expressing dialogue – with oneself as well as with friends, the teacher, family members, imagined characters. There's more to this motif, too, that is worth thinking about. I was struck by the astute distinction made by Linda O'Callaghan, one of the Year 6 teachers, that published work offered her pupils pride in their achievements but private journals offer them pleasure. This is similar to the balance between the individual and the social, but implies rather more about the product of the writing than the process. Both kinds of writing intersect, of course, but are also related to the inner and outer worlds – the monologues and dialogues – offered by the journals. This also links with the strong feature of identity developed through the journals and the roles they allow writers to adopt safely. Whilst any young writer may experience both pride and pleasure in a piece of writing which 'goes public', writing journals offer opportunities for both public pride and private pleasure in writing.

A key feature of the journal work was the satisfaction the children found in playing with language. They played physically with its decoration; experimentally in the topics chosen; in the patterned ways they used font, size, shape and page layout; in the rhymes and rhythms of the language of the journal entries; and in the combinations of colour, shape, sound, space. It is no surprise, of course, since as Lynda and Annette have described, the journals reflect the children's cultural knowledge and experience – or 'capital'. Children know a great deal about many forms of text, particularly those which include sound, voices, intonation, stance, gesture, movement, as well as print and image. These texts have changed the ways in which young readers expect to read, the ways they think and the ways they construct meaning, and are variously reflected in the journals.

The decorative aspects of the journals are particularly interesting and show the multidimensionality of the children's knowledge of language. Ornamented letters are a kind of visual adjective, the direction of the drawings and writing suggests sound and action. Certainly, there is an important element of the aesthetic and even tactile in the journals, all of which raises some questions about how this multimodal knowledge and experience can properly be fostered in the classroom, particularly when there is still a very pressing need for the children to write, straight off, accurate continuous prose in order to achieve well in SATs. As with so many apparent classroom and teacherly dilemmas, the children themselves offer a way forward. Evidence from this project very strongly suggests that the opportunity to play with language and to talk about it, to experiment with different forms and discuss them with friends and teachers, helps young writers distinguish between the occasions when multimodal texts are best for the job, and times when continuous prose would be more suitable.

Social, cultural and professional capital
The children have been 'writing their worlds' in their journals. But the worlds – or domains – of school and home intersect. Using Bourdieu's idea of 'cultural capital' (Bourdieu 1977) the classroom can be seen as a site for overlapping domains of social and intellectual experience or 'capital'. In particular, the journal work has made their literacy capital very visible. For some time it has been clear that children's home and school domains need to be seen much more as overlapping rather than being separate. However, the journal work has also highlighted the importance of the teacher's contribution

to the new cultural capital being built up in the classroom. From my discussions with each of the teachers involved, it became clear that their interests, preferences and strengths were being reflected in the children's journals. Each set of journals not only showed the wealth of the pupils' cultural and literacy capital but, importantly, represented the cultural community of each classroom. It also built more capital – both in developing a classroom environment and in developing the teachers' professional experience. All the teachers involved in the project, and those of us who have had a chance to see the work, have added to our professional capital.

There have been parallel benefits and gains for adults and children. The project has made it very clear that both teachers and children feel greater satisfaction when they have opportunities for choices in their work; when they are supported in taking some risks; when they have opportunities for reflection, self-regulation and review; when their cultural and literacy capital can be recognised and extended; when there are opportunities for discussion and rumination over writing; when there is trust in the classroom/school community.

After any curriculum development project, the teachers involved have to answer some 'hard' questions, for example, in this case, 'How will you use/develop writing journals next year?' Most importantly, the Croydon teachers have already begun to answer 'What have you learned that can inform your future practice?'

The teachers now know that writing journals are:
- a very powerful means of catering for diversity in the classroom;
- a valuable indication of children's different strengths and experience as writers;
- a catalyst for motivation and the sense of a need, rather than a duty, to write;
- a space to move between individual and shared social writing experiences;
- a chance for both public pride and private pleasure in writing.

They also know that the work has spilled over into other areas of their class-room work. The insights gained from using the journals can be used to support more explicit teaching of writing; to provide opportunities for experimenting with the different dimensions of text and discussing these explicitly; and to build on the sense of space which the children show in their journal entries. The teachers' increased professional capital is supported by a knowledge that using journals affords both pride and pleasures, and in any recipe for classroom success, these are two essential ingredients.

REFERENCES

Barrs, M. (1996) 'The New Primary Language Record Writing Scale' in *Language Matters 1995/96*, London: CLPE

Barrs, M. (1988a) 'Drawing a Story: Transitions between Drawing and Writing' pp51-69 in Lightfoot, M.& Martin, N. (eds.) *The Word for Teaching is Learning.* Portsmouth: Heinemann Educational Books

Barrs, M. (1988b) 'Maps of Play' pp101-115 in Meek, M. & Mills, C. (eds.) *Language and Literacy in the Primary School.* Brighton: Falmer Press

Barrs, M. & Cork,V. (2001) *The Reader in the Writer.* London: Centre for Language in Primary Education

Bearne, E. (2002) 'Multimodal narratives' pp 67-73 in Barrs, M. & Pigeon, S.(eds) *Boys and Writing.* London: Centre for Literacy in Primary Education.

Bearne, E. & Kress, G. (2001) Editorial *Reading,* 31 (3) p.89-93

Bernstein, B. (1970) 'Education cannot compensate for society' in *New Society*, 387 p344-347

Bourdieu, P. (1977) *Outline of a Theory of Practice* (trans. By Nice, R.) Cambridge: Cambridge University Press

Brooker, L. (2002) *Starting School – Young Children Learning Cultures.* Buckingham: Open University Press

Csikszentmihalyi, M. (2002) (ed.) *Flow: The Classic Work on How to Achieve Happiness.* London: Rider

DfEE (1998) *The National Literacy Strategy: Framework for Teaching.* London: DfEE

DfEE (1999) *The National Curriculum: Handbook for Primary Teachers in England KS1&2.* London. QCA

Dyson, A.Haas (1997) *Writing Superheroes.* New York: Teachers College Press

Fox, C. (1993) *At the Very Edge of the Forest.* London: Cassell

Gardner, H. (1993) *Frames of Mind The Theory of Multiple Intelligences.* London: Fontana Press

Graham, L. (1999) 'Changing practice through reflection: the KS2 Reading Project, Croydon' *Reading* 33 (3) p.106-113

Graham, L. (2001) 'From Tyrannosaurus to Pokemon: autonomy in the teaching of reading' *Reading* 35 (1) p.18-26.

Graham, L. (2002) 'Teachers as experts in Learning' pp42-53 in Barrs, M. & Pidgeon, S. (eds.) *Boys and Writing.* London: Centre for Literacy in Primary Education

Graham. L (2003) 'Writing Journals: an investigation' *Reading* 37 (1) p.39-42

Hall, N. (1989) *Writing with Reason: The Emergence of Authorship in Young Children.* London: Heinemann

Hollindale, P. (1997) *Signs of Childness in Children's Books.* Stroud.: The Thimble Press

Johnson, A. (1999) unpublished field notes for Diploma in Writing and Action Research. Canterbury Christ Church University College

Johnson, A. (2000) *'The importance of oracy in developing children's writing'* Unpublished Dissertation, Diploma in Writing and Action Research. Canterbury Christ Church University College

King, C. (2001) 'I like group reading because we can share ideas: the role of talk within the literature circle' *Reading,* 35 (1) p 32-36

Marsh, J. & Millard, E. (2000) *Literacy and Popular Culture.* London: Sage Publications

Meek, M. (1999) 'Transitional Transformations'. Conference Address. *Where Texts and Children Meet,* Sept 1999, Homerton College, Cambridge

National Writing Project (1990) *Writing and learning* Walton on Thames. Nelson

Rosen, C. & Rosen, H. (1973) *the Language of Primary School Children.* Middlesex: Penguin.

Street,A.& Barrs,M. (1998) 'Relationships on paper' p9-12 in Barrs, M. & Pigeon, S. (eds) *Boys and Reading.* London: Centre for Language in Primary Education

Vygotsky,L. S. (1978) *Mind in Society: the Development of Higher Order Psychological Processes.* Cambridge, Mass.: Harvard University Press

Fiction
Dodd, L. (1985) *Hairy Maclary from Donaldson's Dairy* London Puffin Books

Grindley, S. (1995) *Knock Knock Who's There?* Middlesex Penguin

Rosen, M. (1999) *Little Rabbit Foo Foo* London Walker Books

Rosen, M. (2001) *Uncle Billy Being Silly* London Penguin

Acknowledgements

The following teachers took part in the Writing Journal Project 2001-2002: Carol Domingo, Vivienne Esparon, Joanne Greenhalgh, Sarah Hayward, Kim Lawrence, Jenny Llewellyn, Irene Napier, Linda O'Callaghan, Pat Parlour, Gaynor Talley. We thank them for their enthusiasm and thoughtful research.

We would also like to thank headteachers from the following schools for their support and encouragement for the Writing Journal Project teachers: Paul Matthews (Byron Primary), John White (Cypress Junior), Michael Brockett (Downsview Primary), Sally George (Ecclesbourne Junior), Jill Hamilton (Gilbert Scott Infants), Evelyn Armstrong (Gresham Primary), John Robinson (Howard Primary), Susan Bain (Purley Oaks Primary), Margaret Liddiard (St. Chad's R.C. Primary), Susan Powell (St. John's C of E Primary), Ann Pendry (St. Mary's R.C. Junior).

Finally, we thank all children in the Writing Journal Project. Published extracts from writing journals are by the following children: Daniel Bhairam, Fabio Carter, Lily De La Haye Earl, Seb Evans Thornton, Joe Foot, Georgia Heffernan, Caroline Locke, Ayushi Patel, Shailen Patel, Ishmael Roberts, Raymond Ssekalongo, Sophie Wells, Dwayne Williams, James Zhu.
We thank them for permission to use these extracts.

Where children have used writing implements such as gel pens, reproduction is less than perfect. We hope this does not detract from your interest in the illustrations. However, we felt it important to use genuine journal entries.

About the Authors

Annette Johnson has worked as a classroom teacher for the past thirteen years after taking her PGCE at the Institute of Education. She is currently an Advanced Skills and Leading Literacy teacher, and teaches a Y6 class in a Croydon primary school. She was a teacher-researcher on the Croydon KS2 Reading Project and the Croydon Writing Project, and achieved a distinction in her Post-Graduate Diploma in Education based on this action-research. In 2000 she was awarded the John Downing Award from UKRA for her work with writing journals.

Lynda Graham is Professional Development Consultant for English in the London Borough of Croydon, and an associate lecturer at Canterbury Christ Church University College. During the last seven years she has run two collaborative action research projects in Croydon, one on the teaching of reading at KS2, and currently a four year project on writing in the primary years. All teacher researchers in these projects achieved accreditation at Advanced Certificate level, and a significant number continued their research for two more years and gained Post-Graduate Diplomas.

UKRA Minibooks Series

Series Editor   Susan Ellis

Past series editors   Alison B. Littlefair, Bobbie Neate, Ros Fisher

Issue number 16:
Children's Writing Journals
Issue Authors:
Lynda Graham and Annette Johnson
Series Editor: Susan Ellis

2003   Published by UKLA
ISBN 1 897638 27 2   United Kingdom Literacy Association.
ISSN 1350-7664   Unit 6 First Floor, The Maltings, Green Drift,
Royston, Herts SG8 5DB England